BEARCUB BIOS

MALALA YOUSAFZAI

CHAMPION FOR GIRLS' EDUCATION

by Rachel Rose

Consultant: Beth Gambro
Reading Specialist, Yorkville, Illinois

BEARPORT PUBLISHING

Minneapolis, Minnesota

Teaching Tips

BEFORE READING

- Discuss what a biography is. What kinds of things might a biography tell a reader?
- Look through the glossary together. Read and discuss the words.
- Go on a picture walk, looking through the pictures to discuss vocabulary and make predictions about the text.

DURING READING

- Encourage readers to point to each word as it is read. Stop occasionally to ask readers to point to a specific word in the text.
- If a reader encounters an unknown word, ask them to look at the rest of the page. Are there any clues to help them understand?

AFTER READING

- Check for understanding.
  - Where was Malala Yousafzai born?
  - What does she do?
  - What does she care about?
- Ask the readers to think deeper.
  - If you met Malala, what question would you like to ask her? Why?

Credits:
Cover and title page, © JStone/Shutterstock and © SAKhanPhotography; 3, © JStone/Shutterstock; 5, © Nigel Waldron/Getty Images; 7, © Veronique de Viguerie/Getty Images; 8-9, © TARIQ MAHMOOD/Getty Images; 10-11, © Veronique de Viguerie/Getty Images; 12, © Sean Drakes/Getty Images; 15, © Handout/Getty Images; 16-17, © WENN Rights Ltd/Alamy Stock Photo; 19, © Karwai Tang/Getty Images; 20-21, © WENN Rights Ltd/Alamy Stock Photo; 22, © JStone/Shutterstock; 23TL, © SDI Productions/iStock; 23TR, © nicomenijes/iStock; 23BL, © flukyfluky/iStock; and 23BR, © l i g h t p o e t/Shutterstock.

Library of Congress Cataloging-in-Publication Data

Names: Rose, Rachel, 1968– author. Title: Malala Yousafzai : champion for girls' education / by Rachel Rose. Description: Minneapolis, Minnesota : Bearport Publishing Company, 2020. | Series: Bearcub bios | Includes bibliographical references and index. Identifiers: LCCN 2019060285 (print) | LCCN 2019060286 (ebook) | ISBN 9781642809787 (library binding) | ISBN 9781642809893 (paperback) | ISBN 9781647470005 (ebook) Subjects: LCSH: Yousafzai, Malala, 1997– Juvenile literature. | Girls—Education—Pakistan—Juvenile literature. | Girls—Violence against—Pakistan—Juvenile literature. | Women social reformers—Pakistan—Biography—Juvenile literature. | Taliban—Juvenile literature. | Pakistan—Social conditions—Juvenile literature. Classification: LCC LC2330 .R68 2020 (print) | LCC LC2330 (ebook) | DDC 371.822095491—dc23 LC record available at https://lccn.loc.gov/2019060285LC ebook record available at https://lccn.loc.gov/2019060286

For more information, write to Bearport Publishing, 5357 Penn Avenue South, Minneapolis, MN 55419.

Printed in the United States of America.

Contents

Youngest Winner Ever!

Malala Yousafzai won the Nobel Peace **Prize**.

She worked hard so girls can go to school.

Malala was just 17.

Den Norske Nobelkomite
har overensstemmende med
reglene i det av
ALFRED NOBEL
den 27 november 1895
opprettede testamente tildelt
Malala Yousafzai
Nobels Fredspris
for 2014
Oslo, 10. desember 2014

Malala's Life

Malala was born in the country of Pakistan.

She has two brothers.

Their father was a teacher.

He taught Malala that boys and girls are **equal**.

Malala when she was 12 years old

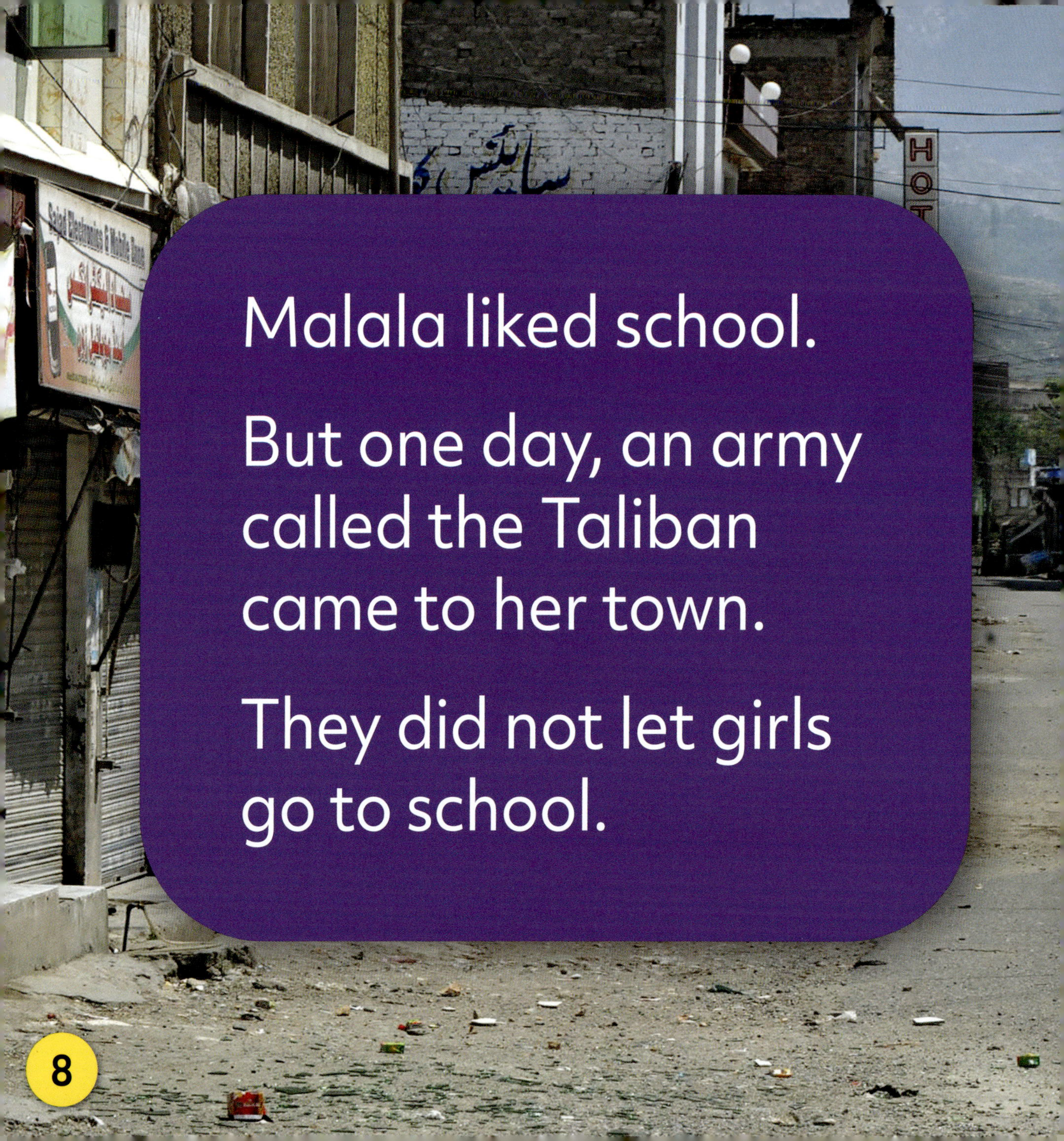

Malala liked school.

But one day, an army called the Taliban came to her town.

They did not let girls go to school.

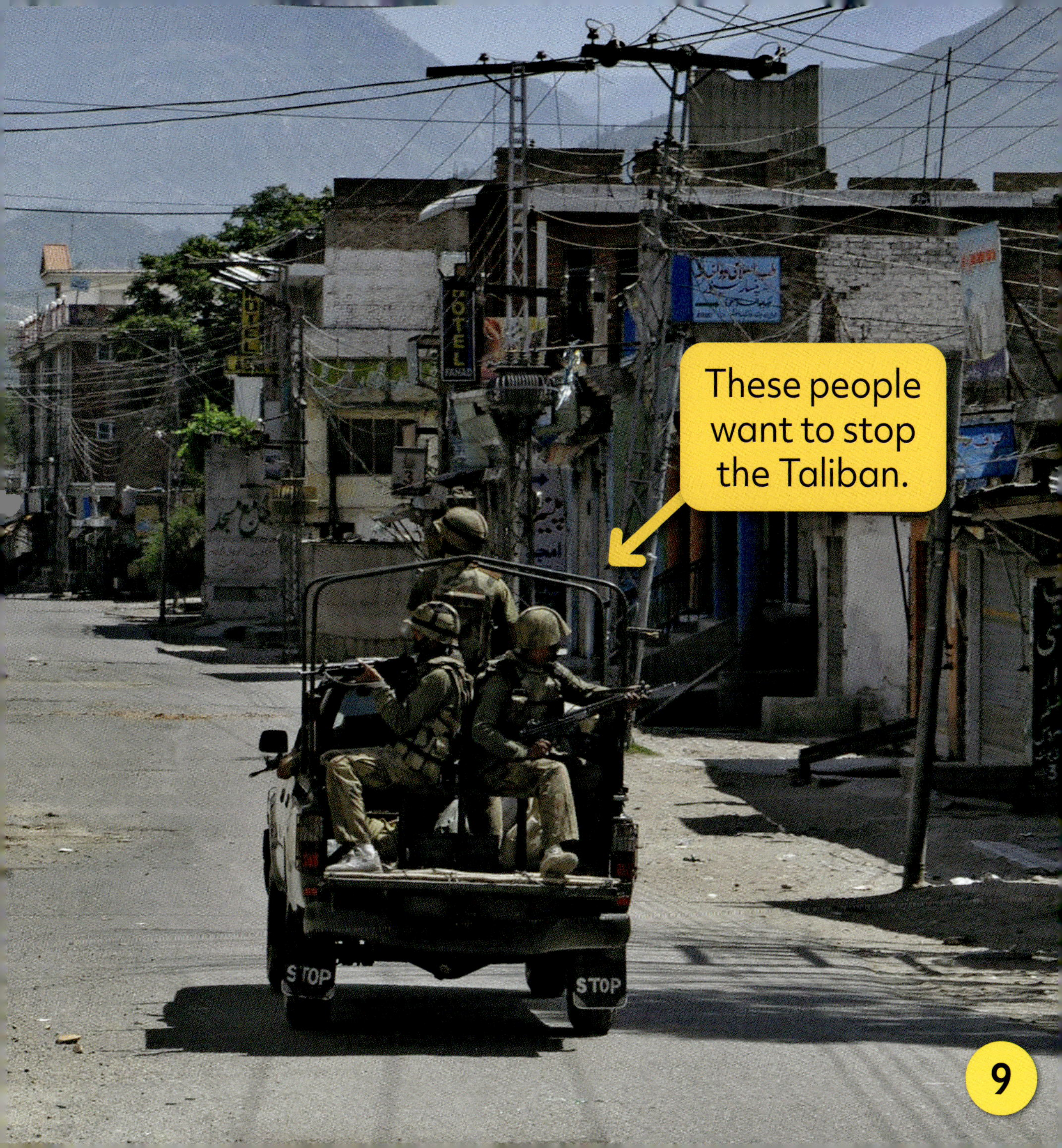
These people
want to stop
the Taliban.
HOTEL
STOP
STOP

Later, girls were able to go to school again.

But there were new rules.

Girls had to cover their heads and faces.

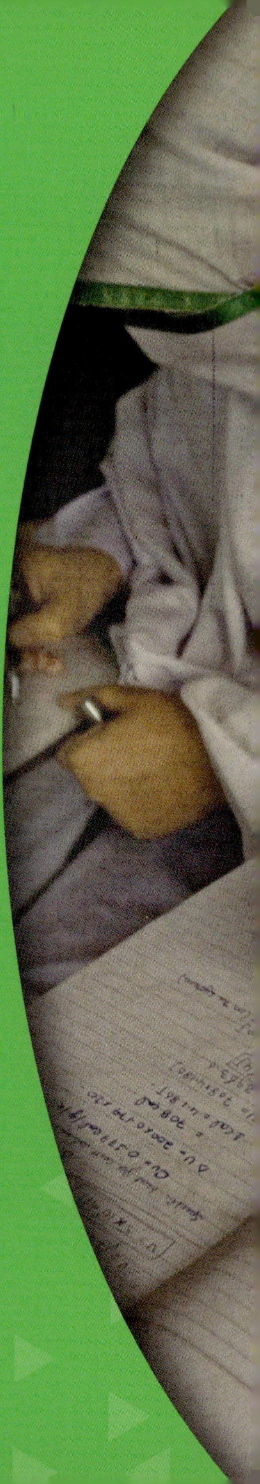

Malala hated the new rules.

She gave a **speech** to tell people how she felt.

She told about her life.

The Taliban did not like what Malala said.

They shot her so she would stop.

Malala was hurt.

Her family took her to England to get better.

Malala in
the hospital

Malala and her family stayed in England.

It was not safe to go home.

Malala was very sad.

But she kept saying the Taliban was wrong.

Malala gave a speech to world leaders.

She spoke about peace and **education** for all girls.

This day was called Malala Day.

WE
DAY

Malala
Malala's father

Malala and her father still work hard.

They help girls around the world.

Malala will keep going for all girls.

Did You Know?

Born: July 12, 1997

Family: Toor (mother), Ziauddin (father), Khushal (brother), Atal (brother)

When she was a kid: Malala wrote her first book about her life. It is called *I Am Malala*.

Special fact: In 2013, Malala was invited to the White House. She met President Obama and his family.

Malala says: "Together, we can create a world where all girls can learn and lead."

Life Connections

Malala spoke out for what she believed in. She kept going even when things got hard. What is something you believe in? How do you work for it?

Glossary

education the act of being at school and learning

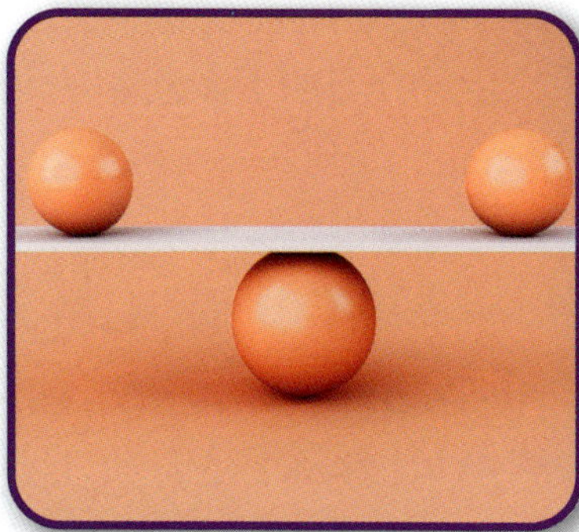

equal the same

prize something won for being the best

speech a public talk

Index

Read More

Moening, Kate. *Malala Yousafzai: Education Activist (Blastoff! Readers: Women Leading the Way).* Minneapolis: Bellwether (2020).

Strand, Jennifer. *Malala Yousafzai (Zoom In on Great Women).* Minneapolis: Abdo Zoom (2017).

Learn More Online

1. Go to **www.factsurfer.com**
2. Enter "**Malala Yousafzai**" into the search box.
3. Click on the cover of this book to see a list of websites.

About the Author

Rachel Rose lives in San Francisco. She grew up in Ireland, where she went to school. Rachel believes that every child around the world has the right to an education.